T0193863

IN SEARCH OF THE HOLY LIFE

REDISCOVERING THE KABBALISTIC ROOTS OF MUSSAR

IRA STONE, BEULAH TREY

IN SEARCH OF THE HOLY LIFE
REDISCOVERING THE KABBALISTIC
ROOTS OF MUSSAR

iUniverse books may be ordered through booksellers or by contacting:

iUniverse
1663 Liberty Drive
Bloomington, IN 47403
www.iuniverse.com
1-800-Authors (1-800-288-4677)

ISBN: 978-1-5320-6980-2 (sc)
ISBN: 978-1-5320-6981-9 (e)

Print information available on the last page.

iUniverse rev. date: 03/05/2019

"Each soul in Yisrael actually contains a portion of all the others…"
Tomer Devorah, Middah Four

To the founding Board of the Center for Contemporary Mussar and board members to come.

Todah Rabah. Thank you.

Your enthusiasm for the Mussar Path we've charted together and your skill at building an organization that can sustain itself is a Mechayeh.

With gratitude we dedicate this book to you.

We wanted to live more meaningful lives; that's where this story begins.

As is the case for increasing numbers of Jews today, our personal Mussar journeys began as a search for more meaning. We sought not only to undergird our Jewish practice with deeper spiritual roots, but were also drawn by the tug of our intuitions that at the very heart of Jewish practice is the practice of living an ethical life. We suspected that by living out that ethical practice — day to day, moment to moment — we could transform ourselves and our relationships with others.

We began our Mussar journey by following the practice instituted by Rabbi Yisrael Salanter in Lithuania in the 19th century: a Mussar practice characterized by discipline and kibbush (restraint) as a path to self-improvement. We turned our inward-facing journeys outward, and applied Mussar's principles to the way we treated other people in our everyday lives. We would focus on the small but critical moments of human interaction and connection that make up our days, and undergird our relationships. This prescription had the potential to serve as an antidote to the narcissism and isolation of our age; and in doing so, could recast the very definition of the Divine for a contemporary audience.

For each of us, this traditional approach was transformative, at first. Yet over time, the "don'ts" of our Mussar practice began to feel confining, suffocating — a narrowing experience, rather than the broadening one we had hoped to achieve. We began to feel mired in the negative, and looked for a way to grow the part of ourselves that yearned to be transformed through actively doing good rather than through restraining our impulses.

Nevertheless, despite our frustrations, when we began teaching Mussar, all we knew from the tradition was kibbush. Thus that's how we taught it for many years.

From the beginning we knew that Rabbi Salantar had talked about something called Tikkun, which we recognized as a specifically Kabbalistic term. Tikkun means repair, and the fact that he gave Kabbalah no significant role in the Mussar curriculum he devised, or in the writings and practice of his earliest and most important disciples, we must conclude that his oversight of Kabbalah was entirely purposeful. To understand further his decision to delete Kabbalah, let's broaden our lens to take in what else was happening in the wider world of Rav Salanter's time. Notably, the growing consequences of the Enlightenment were gradually transforming thought. Since the publication of the meditations of Descartes in 1641, the rule of reason and science had almost entirely supplanted the medieval worldview that had reigned when Kabbalah emerged. Nineteenth century rationalism and its scientific filter had completely overtaken the Jews in Germany, where young Jews were quickly secularizing as a result, and the centrality of Kabbalah as the theology of Judaism of the Middles Ages had been rejected.

From Germany, this Jewish Enlightenment had quickly made its way into Russia and Lithuania. With Enlightenment powering Jewish assimilation in the West and threatening to soon do the same in the East, it is not surprising that despite the mystical preponderance of the existing Mussar literature, the early leaders of the Mussar movement, and Rav Salanter especially, chose to focus on a pragmatically rational, behavioral model that became Mussar.

Kabbalah may have been written out of Mussar in the 19th century, but unearthing its ties and its complementary wisdoms offers a tremendous opportunity to strengthen and transform contemporary Mussar practice. In this light, we can now understand why it is important for us to familiarize ourselves with the Kabbalistic background of Mussar literature. The audience for contemporary Mussar does not have to be protected from secular life, as in Rav Salanter's day. Quite the contrary, people are looking for an *alternative* to secular life: an opportunity to live the holy life.

For us, our discovery of Mussar's formative Kabbalistic texts was what we came to call our "Lech Lecha" moment. In the biblical story of Abraham, he receives a mysterious call that takes him from self-absorption (and living with his idol-worshipping family), to service of the infinite other (the one God). That's how we and our Mussar students felt after endlessly hitting a wall with our laser-focus on kibbush: we realized that simply restraining our Yetzer was not enough, but that we must also move to transforming the energy, or Tikkun.

Like Abraham's journey, it would take us out of our comfort zones and into unfamiliar terrain. We needed new tools for our transition. We chose a new text that presents Mussar in a more explicitly kabbalistic framework. We adopted new terminology to metaphorically describe the inner dynamic of personal transformation. We also created a new protocol for our Vaad work based on the principles of positive psychology and Kabbalah, wherein we created a methodology for transforming moments of interactions with others. It made for a challenging and rewarding practice which we are delighted to share.

The three sections of this book create a framework through which we will explore this intersection of Mussar and Kabbalah. The first section explores Kabbalah to the extent necessary to understand where Mussar texts fit into the larger ideas of some of the major Kabbalistic thinkers. The second part of the book outlines how this Kabbalistic context can create a different and more appropriate Mussar vocabulary for the emerging 21st century Mussar movement. The prospect of creating new language for Mussar is an exciting one, since to expand one's vocabulary is to expand one's very capacity to think; we thus explore how to apply this new vocabulary to strengthen our Mussar practice. The third and final section of this book is a translation and commentary of the first chapter of the most beloved of these Kabbalistic Mussar texts, *Tomer Devorah* — written by 16th century sage Rabbi Moshe Cordovero, known as the Ramak —along with a step-by-step Mussar practice that applies his teachings to day-to-day living.

The Kabbalah

This is not an introduction to Kabbalah in the conventional sense. We will not track the historical development of Kabbalistic ideas, nor will we present the many different metaphoric systems it uses to express profound insights into the nature of reality. Rather, our intent is to sketch those ideas in Kabbalah that enrich our Mussar practice.

From a Mussar perspective, the important question Kabbalah seeks to answer is:

What obligations do human beings have towards each other?

And the corollary question:

Why does human behavior have an impact on the world that is out of proportion to the place of humans in the physical universe?

Related, and intimately linked, are these questions:

What is the source and meaning of human consciousness?

Why are human beings able to enact evil, when evil acts seemingly tear the fabric of a well-functioning world?

The book you are about to read defines a methodology for repairing the tears that human beings inevitably cause in the fabric of the universe. Kabbalah served and can serve as the metaphorical framework to describe this universe, while Mussar provides the method for repair. To understand Mussar within the context of Kabbalah, we must start at the very beginning: with the creation of our world and Being. It is from this vantage point that we can understand the human's place and purpose in creation.

First, a word about the gorgeous metaphors of Kabbalistic literature and its hazards. If we are to embrace Kabbalah as our framework, be aware that the greatest danger of exposure to Kabbalistic literature is reification — that is, treating a metaphor as though it were something concrete. In this context, another word for reification is idolatry. The crucial point to keep in mind, reiterated time and again in Kabbalah, is that all descriptions of reality are metaphors, including descriptions of time and space:

They are human attempts to express the inexpressible. They are never to be taken as literal truth.

To demonstrate the abstract nature and power of Kabbalah's metaphorical language, let's take a moment to examine a foundational phrase, "Ain Sof," which refers to the Divine essence, which existed prior to Creation. Ain Sof literally means "without end" and is sometimes translated as "The Infinite." But these translations are just the beginning of the multifaceted dimensionality that is Ain Sof. Because Ain Sof is not only "without end," but equally without beginning. It refers to the "everything" before there was anything. It is pure mystery, entirely unknowable, unperceivable — and yet everything that will ever exist resides within what we call "the will" of Ain Sof. Understand, there *is* no will of the Ain Sof, but something we *call* the will of the Ain Sof, which precipitates the cosmos. In the language of the Kabbalah, this so-called will of the Ain Sof may also be understood as the "desire" of the Ain Sof.

Mysteriously, this gesture of desire does not change the Ain Sof, but gives rise to the light of the Ain Sof, which begins the world of Being. The Ain Sof is not part of Being or part of the process of Being's becoming. It is not even known by the Being it initiates. In the beginning, all of Being is contained within this light. However, to even use the word "light" is to wrongly suggest a material existence. Remember, light is merely a metaphor, a human expression in limited language of a spiritual reality.

The central metaphor and scaffold of Kabbalah are the sefirot, or emanation, "counting." When we say sefirot are "emanations," we mean the radiations of Divine energy from the Ain Sof into ever-expanding material existence. These emanations make up our experience of the Ain Sof and yet they are not the Ain Sof itself. The closer a sefira is to the Ain Sof, the more refined and spiritual it is. Our world, being furthest from the Ain Sof, is predominantly material. The existence of the sefirot depends upon the Ain Sof "making room" by either contracting or concealing itself — in Hebrew, tzimtzum — depending on the system of Kabbalah one is following.

Tzimtzum is yet another layered concept. Though often translated as "contraction," it also simultaneously means "removal," "concealment" and "revelation." According to most Kabbalists, the process of tzimtzum begins from and is potential in the Light of the Ain Sof. It contains ten dimensions in descending "materiality" or differentiation based on its distance from the Source of Being. At the highest levels there is still nothing resembling materiality, as we understand it. Rather, this serves as a metaphoric structure by which we can describe, in our limited language, the forces of the cosmos. These levels, or sefirot are:

> Keter – Crown
> Hochmah – Wisdom
> Binah – Discernment
> Din – Judgment
> Hesed – Love
> Gevurah – Strength
> Tiferet – Beauty
> Netzah – Eternity or Victory
> Hod – Glory
> Yesod – Foundation

Tzimtzum is a removal of sacred energy; a concealment or hiding that is at the same time a revelation insofar as it reveals the location of the succeeding world. In the same way that the Ain Sof remained unchanged by the act of its desire, so too does each upper world remain unchanged by tzimtzum. By a similar token, each new world is unaware of its source, not in the least because that source had to remove itself in order to make room for creation.

What insights for our lives can we glean from this cosmic poem as we step back from it, making sure that we are reading metaphorically, not literally? Our own reading of this material has yielded both an understanding and a practice that now forms the curriculum of the Center for Contemporary Mussar. First and foremost is the understanding that we live in a universe governed by order and precipitated by a loving desire. We can certainly say that these ten sefirot constitute the attributes that create the universe as we know it, or better, as we would like to imagine it. Its very structure is composed of Wisdom and Discernment, Mercy and Beauty; governed by a reflection of the unknowable Divine who *we* address as God, but who is not to be confused with the Ain Sof, out of which this ideal world emerges.

The Power of People

What is the role of human consciousness in this cosmos and, specifically, the role of the free will that defines that consciousness? We have come to the nexus between Kabbalah and Mussar.

The emanation of the sefirot proceed almost mechanically, with each lower level exhibiting less and less spiritual refinement until the level of materiality is reached. Within each sefira the lowest level, that of Malchut, sends out a line of energy below it, ending in a point. This point is emptied of all Divine energy (ie, tzimtzum as a concealment that is also a revelation). The return of all the sefirot into the space that has just been created produces a material world structured by the nine sefirot, and culminating with the creation of a human being. Or better, a human *form* whose creation in the image of God as described in Genesis signifies that the physical human form in the material world corresponds to the immaterial structure of the entire cosmos and all the sefirotic worlds contained therein. Human beings are the aspect of the system within which is embedded every one of the worlds above them in the order of creation.

The ultimate metaphor for this conception is that the breath of the Divine Ruach enters the human as Neshama and gives it its Being as Nefesh. This Neshama bypasses all of the levels and worlds and enters the human directly from the level of Keter. This miracle, implicit in the entire system from the beginning, essentially turns the system upside down: the lowest and final element to come into being receives the power and, in turn, becomes the source of power, thus sustaining the entire edifice. As Emmanuel Levinas quotes from *Nefesh Ha-Hayyim* in his book *Beyond the Verse*:

> [God], confers upon [human beings] the power to free or stop ('to open or close') thousands of myriads of forces and worlds, on account of all the detail and all the levels of [their] conduct and all [God's] perpetual concerns, thanks to the superior root of [God's] deeds, words and thoughts, as if [humans] too were the master of the forces that command these worlds. (I.3)

Thus, we may say that Being is sustained by the flow of Divine goodness "from above" through the *sefirotic* emanation, and is simultaneously controlled by the deeds, words and thoughts of humans from "below."

The obvious and seemingly — but not really — radical conclusion of all this is that the universe is dependent upon a mysterious partnership between "God" and humans. This idea is strongly implied in the biblical text, is explicitly addressed in Rabbinic literature and is depicted in exquisite detail in Kabbalistic literature. The responsibility of humans for the very existence of Being is both ennobling and terrifying. The tools which humans have at their disposal are mitzvot — the laws and rituals that interrupt self-absorption, the source of sin — and middot, the disciplines by which we come to control that self-absorption and transform it into service of the good of our neighbor. That discipline is called Mussar.

This system of discipline allows a person to continually tap into the transformative experience of direct contact with an essential facet of God. In this way, energy of the Divine is continually transferred to the realm of the human. It is literally imagined as a person's ability to draw down the sustaining goodness from the Source of Being, the Light of Ain Sof. The experience is one of devikut, or attachment to the Source of All. This is the very goal of the system: attaining this bond, wherein the Kedusha, or holiness, of the Divine source directly corresponds to the Kedusha of the human in the cosmic drama.

That people are viewed as having such capacity for power is, as we've said, ennobling. It is also dangerous. Because this highly metaphoric picture contains within it the actual, terrible truth: we are the extensions of God into the world, which we co-create at every moment. Uncovering this truth is the human journey. We are born 'ignorant' of our place in the system. Over the course of a life, there are moments of revelation, moments when we can become aware of our profound obligation to sustain the world. Because we have free will, waking up to this reality is not a given, it is only a possibility.

It is this frightening, destabilizing knowledge — that we are the vessels of God on earth — which is what required Kabbalah to be kept secret and also to be handed down across the generations. The two things that had to be kept secret are first, the extent of human power; and second, that God is not a being, God is a system in which humans play a part. If we humans were to stop doing our part, there is no world for our good actions that are also God's actions, and our evil actions are our repudiation or rejection of the Divine imperative.

The realization of this power can be used for good or evil. The self-absorption of human beings, which we call Yetzer Hara, is the result of humans acting as though we are God, as opposed as an aid to this effort. The next section contains Cordovero's chapter one printed in bold, the distillation of each middah in italics, and our commentary in normal font.

To learn more about our method, we invite you to view the Center for Contemporary Mussar's website and our workbooks.

Tomer Devorah

Introduction

Rabbi Moshe Cordovero was born in 1522 in the Israeli city of Safed into a family of Spanish descent, probably from the city of Cordova; hence the family name. He would eventually, and famously, become known as the Ramak, an acronym made up of the first letters of his title and name. Little is known of his early life or his family of origin, but we know that his primary teacher in normative rabbinic studies was Rabbi Joseph Caro, one of the great mystics of Safed, and author of the authoritative code *Shulchan Arukh*, but Caro's studies with Ramak appear to have been limited to Talmud and Halacha. Ramak was ordained by Rabbi Ya'akov Berav at the age of 18 and worked as a Talmud teacher in Safed.

According to legend, two years later, Ramak was urged by an angelic voice to study Kabbalah. He began to study with his brother-in-law Rabbi Shelomo Alkabez. In addition to being the author of the famous hymn *Lecha Dodi*, Rabbi Alkabez was the head of an active group of Safed Kabbalists and the author of Kabbalistic treatises and commentaries. In the variegated community of mystics in Safed, Ramak mostly eschewed the schools of practical Kabbalah — though he moved among the followers of Isaac Luria — or of wonder-working Kabbalah, in favor of a more speculative, metaphysical Kabbalah. He would study it for the rest of his life. His most important work is the multi-volume *Pardes Rimmonim*, "Orchard of Pomegranates." It is a comprehensive elucidation of all the tenets of Kabbalah. He died on June 25, 1570 at the age of 48.

Our choice of Ramak and specifically *Tomer Devorah* as a Tikkun guide gave us a text that focused on middot and pointed our Mussar journey in the direction of holiness. *Tomer Devorah* explicitly uses kabalistic language unlike our earlier text, Ramchal's *Mesilat Yesharim*, where the kabbalistic influence was hidden.

TOMER DEVORAH

Chapter 1

TEXT: It is proper for a person to emulate the
Creator, for then they will attain the secret of
the Supernal Form in both image and likeness.
For if a person's physical form reflects the
Supernal Form, yet their actions do not, they
falsify their stature. People will say of them:
"Their form is handsome, but their deeds are
ugly." For the essential aspect of the Supernal
Form and Likeness is that they are the deeds of
the Holy Blessed One. Therefore, what good is
it for a person to reflect the Supernal Form in
physical form only if their deeds do not imitate
those of the Creator? Thus, it is proper that a
person's actions imitate the thirteen Supernal
attributes of mercy – functions of the sefirah of
Keter – hinted at in these verses:

> Who is like You, who pardons iniquity and
> forgives the transgressions of the remnant
> of God's heritage? God does not maintain

1

the vehicles to holiness. According to Ramak, the endeavor to embody these thirteen characteristics is the very purpose of life.

The journey begins with the attribute of Mi El Komacha, or "Sufferance," defined as the capacity "to continue to nourish and sustain others as we bear insult beyond understanding." According to Ramak, the key to developing Sufferance is reckoning with the concept of "beyond human understanding." To move beyond human understanding is to act towards others in ways that might ordinarily be seen as counter to our own self-interests.

For the purposes of our Mussar work, we have interpreted this middah and those following in the language that we've adopted: Ruach, Neshama, Nefesh, Ner Tamid. Our ability to act with Sufferance begins when we contemplate the fact that despite our own imperfect behavior, we continue to be nourished and sustained. The constancy of nourishment and sustenance in the language that we have adopted is Ruach (explained above). Ruach holds, surrounds and connects us to each other. This Source of wellbeing in the world is beyond our imagining. It is a goodness that sustains and nourishes us, even if we grow distant from the Source.

Wellbeing is also at the root of what we've called Neshama. Ruach when 'breathed' into a human being is Neshama, as when in Genesis 2:7 God created a living soul by breathing into Adam the breath of life. It is imbued with loving responsibility for the Other, our neighbor. The term Ner Tamid refers to the individual characteristics of Neshama that are expressed as the unique quality of that each person brings to bearing this responsibility.

The Other's experience of our behavior is mediated by the Nefesh. When the Nefesh both holds us in and, at the same time is open to others, the energy of our Neshama, which we've called Yetzer, emerges as Tov (good). When the Nefesh is either too rigid or overly porous, then the Yetzer expresses *Ra* (evil).

Thus, no person ever sins against God without God, at that very moment, bestowing abundant vitality upon them; giving them the power to move their limbs, Yet even though they use this very vitality to transgress, God does not withhold it from them. Rather, The Holy Blessed One suffers this insult and continues to enable their limbs to move. Even at the very moment that a person uses that power for transgression, sin, and infuriating deeds, the Holy Blessed One bears them patiently.

Sin, or the power to choose to serve the self at the expense of another person, occurs when the boundary of the Nefesh becomes rigid and constrains the Neshama, causing Yetzer to be expressed as Ra. It is a natural consequence of the unconscious choices we make, most of which relate to the seemingly necessary and legitimate decisions to defend ourselves. Evil results from the mistaken notion that we need to protect ourselves from threat in order to ensure our survival. But despite whatever evil the Yetzer HaRa performs, the sustaining power of life is not denied us. Despite the logical possibility that evil actions will result in the withdrawal of the life force, we know that it does not. We cut ourselves off from an ever-sustaining flow.

One cannot say, God forbid, that God cannot withhold God's benevolence from a person, for it is within God's power to shrivel up a person's arms or legs instantly, just as God did with Yaravam. Yet even though it is within God's power to withdraw vitality, and God could argue, "Since you sin against Me, sin with that which belongs to you, not with that which belongs to Me," God does not withhold God's

goodness. God bears the insult and continues to bestow God's power and benevolence on humans. Such insult and forbearance thereof defy description.

Yaravam was a Biblical king whose evil caused the tortuous death of all of his descendants. Metaphorically, this story, like many in the Biblical canon, emphasizes the easily threatened nature of the Nefesh. The reality is that human beings regularly act in ways that threaten our very ability to survive. This self-destructive capacity of human beings is in stark contrast to the Source of wellbeing that is ever-present. This is because this attribute is beyond human understanding. Imitating this kind of sufferance in the face of otherwise intolerable behavior is the first level of *imitatio Dei*.

For this reason, the ministering angels refer to the Holy Blessed One as the long-suffering King. This is the meaning of "Who is God like You" – "You, God, are kind and benevolent, possessing the power to exact revenge and claim what is rightfully Yours, and yet You are patient and tolerant until people repent."

The intention of sufferance is not suffering. The Holy One never suffers. Infinite wellbeing enters the Nefesh with the forceful command to serve the Other. We are no longer satisfied with simply restraining the Yetzer, which is the first stage of Mussar practice, (kibbush). Now, we actively transform the Yetzer from Ra to Tov (Tikkun). Sufferance, the first Tikkun middah, provides us with a method. Even when a person is insulted to the degree mentioned above, one should not withdraw benevolence.

Thus the attribute of sufferance is one that humans should emulate even when they are insulted to such a degree as mentioned above, they should still not withdraw their benevolence from the recipient.

The ascent to Kedusha begins by practicing the quality of sufferance. To apply this middah to our lives, Ramak provides a foundation for living the well-lived life, beginning with the concept that *we are in charge of how we respond to the circumstances around us.* And when we are challenged by Others in our lives, this middah offers a prescription for how to keep our Nefesh semi-permeable.

There are two important notions set forth in the middah. The first is that being good and sustaining the others in our lives, both physically and emotionally, is nourishing for ourselves, regardless of how the other person acts towards us. The second idea is that there is a Divine goodness that operates beyond comprehension. Even when we interpret an act of the other as an insult, Divine goodness requires that we respond beyond the limits of human understanding, which is to continue to nourish and sustain the other regardless.

To which we must first ask ourselves: What *is* Divine goodness?

Our answer is: the best of yourself, which is acting in congruence with your "Ner Tamid statement" — the words and phrases with which you describe your personal aspirational manifestation of divinity. The Ner Tamid statement is an ever-evolving effort to use language to focus your energy on maintaining a semi-permeable Nefesh boundary. With practice, you will develop an ever more precise, ever more clear experience of how your own Ner Tamid can continue to grow and inhabit the space Ramak defines as "continue to nourish and sustain with Divine goodness."

Once we have achieved this first step to the best of our abilities, we are ready for our second question: When we feel insulted by the other person, can we *stop* nourishing and sustaining them?

It is human nature to experience an insult as pain. Our first instinct may be to close down and distance ourselves from the other person; or the opposite, to overly open by trying to understand our reaction, or the other person's motivation until we almost disappear. Both of these are instances of self-absorption and will necessarily create Ra energy. Ramak uses the model of the Divine to indicate that we can go beyond mere human nature and act in holiness when we resist the impulse to explain, and instead direct our energy to nourish and sustain the other.

MIDDAH TWO: TOLERANCE

Nosei Avon (Who Bears Iniquity)

See the person's Yetzer HaRa as separate from them, and
Trust in repentance

This attribute is greater than the previous one, for when a person transgresses, a destructive creature is created. As stated in the Mishnah, "Whoever commits a single transgression acquires against oneself a single accuser" who stands before the Holy Blessed One and states, "So-and so made me."

Ramak introduces us to the next Tikkun middah by stating that it exceeds the grandeur of the one before. In this way, he conveys that the middot build on each other, each opening a path to the next. In this instance, the middah of Tolerance is greater than Sufferance in that Sufferance focuses on the self 'bear[ing] the assault'; there is no attention paid to the Other who committed the assault. But with Tolerance, our field of vision expands to include the perpetrator. This movement of focus to an other opens the space within ourselves for Neshama to expand into.

Ramak reminds us that it is not up to us (and not the way of the Holy One) to give up on any Other, even one who sins against us. To reach holiness, we practice separating the evil from the evildoer. For as long as it takes, we hold onto the inevitability that the sin will be expunged from this universe where wellbeing reigns. We hold our precious Other person as lovingly as they are held by the Holy One. Who are we to treat them any differently?

With this second middah, Ramak wants us to answer the nagging question on our path to holiness: How do we relate to sinners, sin and evil? For Ramak, humans create evil as a byproduct of our self-absorption. At least twice in this chapter, Ramak reminds us that despite evildoers' sins, the Holy One does not deprive them of breath, food or any of the building blocks of life. At this point Ramak wants us to accept:

- That humans sin, and;
- That evil is alive and distinct from the sinner, and its consequences beyond the control of the sinner. Remember, "sinning" is an inevitable aspect of being human, as it is an expression of a constrained Yetzer and a rigidified or overly-porous Nefesh

Considering that no being in the world exists except by virtue of the fact that the Holy Blessed One grants it life, how does the force of destruction stand before God? The strict letter of the Law would justify that the Holy Blessed One should claim, "I do not nourish destructive creatures! Go to the one who made

you and derive your sustenance [there]." Then the destructive creature would immediately descend and take the life of the sinner, or cut the sinner off from the sinner's spiritual source, until the destructive being would cease to be.

When we can separate the sinner from the evil, we are in a moment of transcendence. Metaphorically, the evil is a creature born out of a sinful act. This imagined creature receives its nourishment and sustenance from the Holy Blessed One. As we have learned, another name for the source of this nourishment is Ruach. Ruach sustains all, regardless of our actions. The cosmos, as it were, does not withhold its energy from us when we act out of our self-absorption, even when those actions are extreme. Since Ruach continues to sustain us in Divine love, no matter what, it is always possible for us to open ourselves to this nourishment. Another way of saying this is that Tikkun (repentance) is always possible.

> **Nevertheless, the Holy Blessed One does not make this claim. Rather, God bears the sin and endures it and just as God sustains the entire world, God sustains this destructive creature until one of three things happens:**
>
> **The sinner repents, destroying or nullifying the destructive creature by acts of penance,**
>
> **The righteous Judge nullifies it through the suffering or the death of the sinner,**
>
> **The sinner descends to Gehinom to pay the debt.**

> **This may also be the explanation of Cain's plea, "Is my sin too great to bear?" (Bereshit 4:13), which our sages interpreted as: "You bear and desire and nourish and sustain the entire world! Is my sin so severe that You cannot bear it [i.e., sustain the destructive creature] until I repent and rectify the sin?"**

> **Thus, that God nourishes and sustains the evil creature created by the sinner until the sinner repents represents the great quality of tolerance.**

Practicing Tolerance means moving our focus from the evil to increasing our capacity to pardon the sinner. In Ramak's metaphor, the sin becomes a creature that is forbidden by God from taking revenge on the creature's creator. This gives the sinner time to repent. In our idiom, this means giving the sinner time to move from a closed or overly porous Nefesh to expressing Yetzer HaTov. Ramak asserts three possibilities, all of which culminate in the expression of Yetzer HaTov. Either the sinner transforms and achieves a semi-permeable Nefesh, or the sinner dies and the consequences of the Ra energy dissipates; or the Ra has become so strong that it is left to the next generations to transform it from Ra to Tov.

By implication, our responsibility is to stop focusing on the Ra, and instead increase our capacity to hold this Other person in love. This takes time. Time allows our Neshama to once again fill the space between us and the perceived evildoer. The practice of Tolerance gives time for the Neshama of the Other to experience the inevitable consequences created by their self-absorption. We wait, confident that the evil will be expunged. Three possibilities exist:

• The sinner will transform the *Yetzer* from *HaRa* to *HaTov*;

- The sinner will die, and thus the sin will no longer exist in this world of wellbeing; or
- Ramak informs us that in some cases the 'evil creature' lives on, past the death of its creator. This is how we understand the classical concept of *Gehinom*. The sin lives on indefinitely and continues to work its evil among those who live after the sinner. It becomes the living's responsibility to transform the sin, since the sinner is already gone.

It is thus with tremendous Tolerance that God nourishes and sustains the evil creature created by the sinner until repentance. From this, people should learn to what extent they, too, should be tolerant and bear the yoke of their fellows and their evil, even though those transgressions may be of such magnitude that the harm remains. They should tolerate one who sinned against them until the sinner mends their[1] ways or the sin disappears of its own accord. The same applies to other situations.

The middah of Tolerance guides us to a higher level of Kedusha than the previous middah. When we apply the first middah, we work on bearing the felt experience of an insult without using our minds to understand. We do not distinguish between whether we were or weren't insulted; it is enough that we *feel* insulted.

With Tolerance, we move our attention from the felt experience of an insult to the reality of sin and evil itself. When practicing Tolerance, we are face-to-face with the reality that even when an evil has been committed against us, Kedusha requires us

---

[1] Of all the ways of managing the gendered language of English and the gendered language of Ramak, we have chosen to use the plural despite it being ungrammatical.

to continue to nourish and sustain. The application of this middah gives us an opportunity to exercise our Ner Tamid in order to maintain our semi-permeable Nefesh boundary in the presence of evil and sin. Ramak provides three steps.

1. *Continue to nourish and sustain, even in the face of evil acts.*
2. *See the person's Yetzer HaRa as separate from them, and*
3. *trust in repentance.*

To keep our Nefesh boundary semi-permeable in the presence of evil, we are asked to take the long view. We are asked to cultivate the ability to let go of the fact of evil and of evildoers and, rather, trust that good will prevail. We trust that eventually, the sinner will resolve the evil through *Tikkun*, nullification or *Gehinom*. The deep practice of Tolerance is that of cultivating the ability to let go of the outcome, while at the same time trusting that the only possibility is a good one. No other action is required. Our work is to support the sinner until that person faces his or her sin. Notice it is not ours to do anything to hasten this person's reckoning. It is not ours to assist the sinner in mending his or her ways. Our responsibility is "simply" to "sustain and nourish" the person.

MIDDAH THREE: FORGIVENESS

L'mi she'oveir al Pesha ("And Passes over Transgression")

Be the purifying waters and
Wash away the sins of the other

The greatness of this middah is that the pardon does not come at the hands of an agent, but directly at the hands of the Holy Blessed One. As is written (Psalms 130:4), "For with you there is forgiveness, etc." And what is this "forgiveness?" That God washes away the sin, as is written (Isaiah 4:4), "God has washed away the excrement of the daughters of Zion etc." And it is also written (Ezekiel 36:25), "And I will sprinkle upon you clean water, etc." In other words, passing over transgression is

**like sending an ablution that passes over the
transgression and washes it away.**

Unlike the first two middot, this third middah does not remind
us to "nourish and sustain in Divine goodness." It is now assumed
that establishing ourselves in this Matzav Ruach (frame of mind/
heart) is an unending obligation. We turn to this middah when
our Other's Nefesh boundary is rigid or overly porous. When we
practiced Kibbush we became aware of how the Ra energy of our
Other's closed Nefesh caused us to move out of semi-permeability.
Now in Tikkun, our other's changed Nefesh awakens us to the
possibility of being the agents of Divine forgiveness. Because they
awakened us, we know we are responsible to forgive, regardless
of their actions. This middah uses a water-based metaphor to
illustrate how we are energetically part of the Other's complete
purification. The energy is continuous and works to smooth
obstacles not by force but by constancy.

With this middah, Ramak elucidates the mechanics of
forgiveness. According to Ramak, the attribute of Forgiveness is
even greater than the ones that come before. Why? Because in this
middah we learn that we are the agents who forgive the Other for
whatever harm their burdens caused them to inflict, which can
lead to their Tikkun. Through a series of biblical verses, Ramak
defines "forgiveness" as an unmediated act. When we forgive, we
embody the Divine and channel Divine energy into our human
experience. Our forgiveness *is* God's forgiveness. Ramak goes one
step further in his explication of the concept of the unmediated
nature of pardon. He teaches that forgiveness requires that the
one who was wronged be the one who forgives.

This conception of forgiveness continues the ascent to
holiness. At the beginning of our Mussar journey we learned to
recognize the experience of a closed or overly porous Nefesh, and
the effects of the Ra energy it generates. We became aware that
often our Nefesh was stimulated by the other's closed or porous

Nefesh – or we came to know that when we were in the presence of other people's burdens our Yetzer was stimulated into Ra. We also began to know that when we felt our own Yetzer HaRa we were in the presence of another's burden. Now, as we become aware of our Yetzer HaRa, we know we are obligated to take up our unique responsibility for the other person.

We now know that when another is in their Yetzer HaRa their Nefesh boundary is overly constrained through rigidity or because it is overly porous. For Ramak, the obligation to forgive is synonymous with our responsibility to know that the Neshama of the Other is constrained. We are instructed to experience the consequences of the other's burden as excrement that covers the person and masks their goodness. Through our loving presence, and like the steady sprinkling of clean waters, we wash away the filth and allow the goodness to be visible again. Thus Ramak reminds us that only we who have experienced the "excrement" firsthand can be the ones to "clean" it.

> **And behold, this is exactly what a person should be like, not to say: "Is it for me to rectify what so-and-so has sinned against or perverted?" One should not say so, for a person sins and the Holy Blessed One, not through an agent, rectifies the crookedness and washes away the excrement of the person's sin. It follows that a person will be ashamed to go back to sinning, since it is the King who washes the filth off the garments.**

This act of direct forgiveness is necessary to soften the Nefesh boundary of the sinner. The possibility exists that the person who has acted out of extreme self-absorption will be so surprised by this approach to forgiveness that the shock can effectively interrupt the sinner's self-absorption. Stimulated by engagement with another, this can be the beginning of the self-absorbed person's Nefesh return to semi-permeability. His or her always-present and always-potential Neshama may then be encouraged to flow. The sinner may then refrain from returning to sin.

This middah is useful when our Other is acting out their Yetzer HaRa by targeting us. The ability to enlarge our Ner Tamid to include the flow of "purifying water" so that we take up a role in forgiving those who target us with their Yetzer HaRa energy is the third step in our journey to transcendence.

MIDDAH FOUR: INTIMACY

LeSher'it Nachalato (For the Remnant of His Heritage)

Know their pain
Rejoice in their good fortune

The Blessed Holy One acts toward the people of Yisrael in this way: Asking: "What shall I do for them who are my near-ones? I have with them a family relationship." For they are the "spouse" of the Holy Blessed One; they are also called "daughter," "sister" and "mother." As our sages explain: And it is written, "The People of Yisrael are the near-ones (relatives) of the Holy One." The Divine has an actual familial relationship with them, and they are as children. This, too, is the meaning of the words sher'it, remnant or heritage. And what does God say? "If I punish

> them, the pain is mine." As it is written: "In all
> their pain God (lo) is afflicted." The word "Lo"
> is written with an aleph implying that their pain
> extends to the level of Keter called pelah. Aleph
> has the same letters as pelah referring to the
> sefira of Keter and how much more so to the
> level of the "dual visage," Tiferet and Malchut,
> through which the world is mainly conducted.
> For it is read "lo" with a vav signifying that the
> pain is God's. This is also the intention of what
> is written, "And God's soul could not tolerate
> the misery of Israel" for God cannot tolerate
> their suffering and disgrace since they are the
> remnant of God's heritage.

The procession of the Tikkun middot moves us forward on
the journey to ever more sublime embodiments of holiness, this
time through the lens of intimacy. First we learned the stance of
holiness "continues to nourish and sustain in Divine goodness."
Then we learned the ways we could let ourselves off the hook for
maintaining that stance, such as when we are insulted, or when
the Other acts from their Ra. We learned to trust in the power of
holiness to transform and purify. Now with this fourth middah,
as we begin to free ourselves from our instinctual need to judge
others, we are ready to connect with others. We are ready for
intimacy.

The name of this fourth middah is called the "Remnant of
God's Heritage" in the original text, but we choose to call it
"Intimacy." It is a guide for how to be present with everyone, in
every situation, no matter how he or she acts — whether they
embody their Ra or Tov. As with all Tikkun middot, preparation
is key. For when we actually come into contact with others, our
success in embodying this middah is our ability to keep our

Neshamah shining through a semi-permeable Nefesh, no matter the state of the other person's Yetzer.

For the middah of Intimacy, Ramak explores the close relationship that exists between the Divine and humanity through a brilliant series of metaphors related to familial relationships. The Hebrew term used to describe the family, Krovi, which comes from the root of KRV or "approach/come close," further cements the metaphor. Ramak first describes the bond between the Holy One and humanity in gender-neutral terms ("spouse"), then in specifically feminine terms ("sister, mother and daughter") Following Rabbinic tradition, Ramak uses this feminine language to indicate Divine compassion — a profound form of intimacy between God and humanity. Thus Ramak teaches that when human beings cultivate intimacy with one another, they are emulating the Divine, and in this way they experience intimacy with each other and the Divine.

An essential element of this intimate relationship is illuminated by the third and definitive verse, taken from Isaiah: "In all their pain God is afflicted." In this metaphor of God's empathy with human pain, we are to understand one essential aspect of how intimacy is possible in our human relationships. It teaches that our pain is an aspect of God's Being. Rashi believed this so thoroughly that when commenting on Exodus 24:10, which depicts God as sitting on a throne undergirded by a brickwork of sapphire, Rashi explains that the brickwork is constituted of Israel's pain. When a human is in pain, there is the potential for a unique bond of intimacy with another human being, which is a manifestation of intimacy with the Divine. From this we learn that we bring the Divine into the world when we respond to the pain of another. Aren't times of trouble and pain moments of connection with the Divine for many? And isn't the experience of the Divine defined by experiences with caring others? While this is not the only path to feeling the presence of the Divine, Ramak reminds us of the quality of intimacy available when there is pain.

Through an ingenious series of word plays, Ramak assigns intimacy to the highest level of creation identified in Kabbalistic teachings, called Keter (crown).

The Kabbalah imagines that the breath breathed into human beings (Neshamah) emanated from the highest of spherot, Keter, *directly* into humanity (and not via the other sefirot on the way down). Since that breath of life was breathed into Adam, the first human — not the first Jew — Ramak redefines Bnai Yisrael as referring not just to Jews, but to all people. Intimacy's home within Keter suggests a universalist translation of Bnai Yisrael as encompassing all human beings.

A person should behave the same way towards his fellow, since all Bnai Yisrael are related to each other, since all souls are united, and each soul contains a part of all others. This is why nothing can compare to a multitude that does a mitzvah (Torat Kohanim 26:8). The reason is that they are all united and complement one another. And thus, our Sages z"l explain (Brachot 47b), regarding one who is counted among the first ten to arrive at the Beit Haknesset (synagogue), that even if one hundred come after, the first ten receive an reward equivalent to them all. "One hundred" is to be understood literally, since the souls of each of the first ten are included in each other, thus there are ten times ten, which equals one hundred. And since each soul includes all of the others every one of them is a combination of one hundred souls. Therefore, even if a hundred come after him, his reward equals all of the hundred. This is also why "Bnai Yisrael are guarantors thus responsible and liable for one another" (Shevuot, 39a), since

each soul in Yisrael actually contains a portion of all the others, and when an individual sins, she blemishes her own soul and also the portion of every other Israelite that she possesses within herself. It is this portion that requires her friend to be a guarantor for her. Hence, all Yisrael are related to one another.

Ramak explains that human consciousness is plural — that is, the Ruach is a part of every soul; or more figuratively, Ruach is the substance that makes up every soul, and all Ruach is one. From this we can extrapolate that the foundational task of all spiritual life is to recognize and acknowledge the interconnected nature of Being. This recognition and acknowledgment are but the first steps and the work of the preceding middot.

The monumental leap of faith embodied in this fourth middah is internalizing this realization so that the needlessly rigidified boundaries of our Nefesh become semi-permeable. The Nefesh's semi-permeable boundary contains both our individuality and maintains our oneness with all. This awareness allows the Neshamah, whose source is Keter, to beam through the Nefesh. The practice of mitzvot is what awakens our recognition of our infinite obligation to serve the Other who is "as our self." It is through this recognition and practice that we increase the Neshamah's flow.

Therefore, it is proper to desire the benefit for one's fellow, view one's neighbor's good [fortune] in a positive way, and cherish one's friend's honor as one's own – for the friend is actually oneself! And for this reason, we are commanded to "Love your fellow as yourself" (Vayikra 19:18). Furthermore, it is proper that one should be pleased with the integrity of

one's fellow, and should never speak ill or be desirous of one's fellow's disgrace, just as the Holy One, desires neither our disgrace nor our suffering, because of our relationship; so too, a person should not be desirous of the fellow's disgrace, suffering, or downfall. Rather, one should be pained by it as if she herself were actually suffering that same pain or rejoicing in the person's good fortune as if he were enjoying that same good fortune.

To imitate the Divine is to know the pain of another as our own pain. Just as the Divine breathes the possibility of goodness into us, we also rejoice in the good fortune of the other. This is the experience of "You shall love your fellow as yourself." This is also the definition that Ramak posits for Yisrael. It is for this reason the Ramak speaks of "Yisrael" rather than "Adam." Adam is humanity, unaware of living under the yoke of infinite obligation, unaware of a connection to Ruach, unaware of the potential for good inherent in Neshamah and most vitally, unaware of the joy possible in service. Adam represents humanity unaware of its obligation to serve the other. The moment humanity recognizes this obligation (mitzvah) is referred to as the "revelation at Sinai," which is synonomous with the making of Bnai Yisrael.

Our obligation towards others is to see pain when we encounter our Other's Yetzer turned to Ra. The middah does not call on us to experience or get lost in the Other's pain. Instead, the middah calls on us to know the Other's grief as his or her experience of disconnectedness, alienation and separation from Others and from the Source of All. This is the only reason Ra is possible. As we feel intimate with this Other, we remind ourselves of our confidence in transcendence, in the ultimate softening of the other's Nefesh. For we know that allowing our Yetzer to flow and embody Tov in the face of the Other's pain is the act of intimacy this situation requires.

When in the presence of someone acting from their Yetzer HaRa, the middah calls on us to resist any pull to attend to the pain itself. Rather we are asked to remember that we also know this kind of pain; we know it from our own experience and we know it exists more generally. In this way it is possible to know the pain without feeling pain, to know disconnection without being disconnected. The act of intimacy is the capacity to be present to the human experience of an Other while at the same time keeping our own Neshama flowing through a semi-permeable membrane.

Similarly, this middah is a guide to being with others when they embody Yetzer Hatov, which really is the best of fortunes. When we encounter someone else's Tov with our own Tov, the goodness is multiplied. In this way, anyone's good fortune is our very own. Yetzer grows brighter in this shared space.

MIDDAH FIVE: TENDER CURIOSITY

Lo HeHazik L'ad Apo (God does not
retain God's wrath eternally)

Replace anger with tender curiosity and re-experience the relationship

This is yet another Divine middah, that even
when a person persists in sinning, the Holy
One, Blessed Be, does not persist in retaining
anger. And even when God does retain anger, it
is not forever. Rather, God allows God's anger
to abate even when the person does not repent;
as we find in the days of Yeroboam, son of Yoash,
that the Holy Blessed One restored the border
of Israel (Melachim B 14:26). Though they were
unrepentant idol worshippers God had mercy
upon them. Why did God have mercy upon

28

them? Because of this quality of not retaining God's anger forever. On the contrary, God allows God's anger to lose its force and though the sin still lingers God does not punish but ever longs, compassionately, for the person's repentance. Hence it is written: "For I will not contend for ever, neither will I bear grudge" (Tehillim 103:9). For the Holy Blessed One shows both severity and tenderness to Israel for their benefit.

So far the Ramak's middot guide us to reach beyond our typical responses to our Nefesh closing or becoming overly porous. We are asked to continue to nurture and sustain in Divine goodness, even when insulted; even when the other goes so far as to do evil. We are asked to drop our judgments and to cultivate intimacy with others. This middah assists us with the most common emotion we feel – anger – and its psychological doppelganger, resentment. In the previous middah we are guided to "know the pain or rejoice in the good fortune." By making the next middah "Tender Curiosity," Ramak intimates that as we work to imitate the Divine, inevitably we will have to contend with our anger and resentment.

Ramak has two messages for us about anger. First, anger is inevitable in our dealings with other people. Second, we always retain the possibility of diffusing anger. It is through this dual process of anger flaring and diffusing that we come to know the position of our Nefesh: rigid, semi-permeable or porous. In anger, our Nefesh is either rigid or porous, as we are either closed off or we are entirely fused with others and thus closed off to ourselves. As anger diffuses, our Nefesh regains its semi-permeability and we can once again experience connection.

Anger is a product of a constrained or porous Nefesh that results in Yetzer HaRa. If we are agile, anger can provide us a wake-up call. That is, if we respond to the awakening that anger offers, we come to know that the flare-up of anger is an early signal that we are acting out our Ra Yetzer.

How do we do this? Once again Ramak calls on us to imitate The Holy Blessed One.

This is a fitting middah with which a person should conduct himself towards his fellows. Even if one is permitted to reprimand her friend or her children severely, and they would accept the rebuke, this is no reason to intensify the reprimand and persist in anger, though she was angered. This applies even where such anger is permissible: for instance, in the case expounded by the Rabbis on the verse: "When you see the donkey of someone you hate lying under its burden" (Shemos 23:5). They explain that this enmity refers to the person who sees his neighbor commit a sin but when there is no other person present so that he cannot be testified against in a Court of Law. In this case it is permitted to hate the sinner for the offence but, nonetheless, the Torah says: "Azov ta'azov immo ('Thou shalt surely be of help')," explained by the Rabbis to mean: "You shall leave aside that [anger] which is in your heart." It is a religious duty to encourage lovingly, and, perhaps, this way of dealing with the person will succeed. This is the very quality of which God has spoken: "God retains not God's anger forever."

Thus in the realm of human society, two important goals of spiritual development are, first, the ability to allow our anger to lose its force by waking us up and, second, to then turn our attention outward. This curiosity, especially when softened by tenderness, is the antidote to anger. We cannot be curious and encouraging of others while we are simultaneously angry with them. Once we have loosened the anger, we turn to our fellow with a curiosity that is a mix of loving detachment and concern: true interest in another.

In day-to-day life, this middah teaches us to experience our anger as a signal that something has occurred that we either didn't expect, didn't understand or is different from that to which we are accustomed. The anger is a deformed Yetzer in response to this difference, our Nefesh's becoming rigid or porous an entirely human reaction. This middah reminds us to cultivate gratitude for the alarm bell of our anger and quickly move instead to curiosity about what we do not know or understand. When we remember to be curious, we embody our Ner Tamid. Practicing this middah means cultivating the capacity to be curious about what happened. We know we are truly practicing the middah when another tells us their truth that is different from ours, and we accept their experience as also true.

MIDDAH SIX: KINDNESS

Ki Chafetz Chesed Hu (For God desires kindness)

When you are wronged and legitimately angry
Remember your innate desire for kindness
Allow one good quality of the other to penetrate you

The next passage requires an introduction. Ramak's commentary is based on Ezekiel's mysterious vision of the creatures that support the Divine Chariot. He describes them as having four faces: human, lion, ox and eagle. He imposes this vision onto the Keruvim, or angelic faces that were atop the altar in the Temple. Beneath the altar fire there was a wheelwork (galgal - probably to draw water from an underground well) in which the officiant could cool the coals collected from the altar before disposal. According to Ezekiel, the angel Gavriel is directed to use those collected coals above the water works (i.e. before they have been cooled) to destroy Jerusalem.

We have already explained elsewhere (Pardas Rimonim, Shaar Heichalos Chapt. 5) that there is a holy chamber where angels are standing by to receive the acts of loving kindness that people perform in this world. And when the attribute of strict judgment accuses Bnai Yisrael, these angels immediately display those acts of kindness, and the Holy Blessed One has mercy upon Bnai Yisrael, since God is desirous of their kindness. And even though they may be guilty, God has mercy on them if they granted kindness to one another. This can be compared to the time of the Destruction of the Holy Temple, when it was said to the angel Gavriel: "Go in between the galgal, beneath the keruv, and fill your hands with burning coals from among the keruvim, and throw them on the city..." (Yechezkel 10:2). For Gavriel is the angel of judgment and strictness, and was given permission to receive the powers of judgment from the fire on the Altar, which is between the galgal, below the keruvim. This is judgment according to the strictness of malchut, which became so severe that it sought to destroy everything and uproot the core of Bnai Yisrael, because they had incurred the penalty of annihilation. However, the passage continues (ibid. 10:8), "The form of a hand appeared under the wings of the keruvim," meaning that the Holy Blessed One said to Gavriel, "They grant kindness towards one another" (Vayikra Raba 26:8). So even though they were guilty, they were saved, and a remnant of them was left. The reason for this is due to the middah

of "God is desirous of kindness," meaning – the kindness that Bnai Yisrael grant to one another. And God reminds them, the Heavenly court, of this righteous aspect, even though, in other aspects, they are not righteous.

What happens to the actions of people? Ramak uses the full force of the story and metaphor to remind us of the fundamental Jewish understanding that human actions shape the cosmos — and that one human being's actions profoundly impact the cosmos of another human being, affecting their thoughts and actions.

In this cosmic constellation there is what we might call a gravitational "pull" that maintains the world's "orbit." That pull is the pull of kindness. This gravitational pull of kindness mysteriously emanates from and is part of the substance of Ruach. Ramak's metaphor of angels deploying the acts of kindness that we also perform to sustain and nourish us exemplifies this "pull." Kindness is not described as a gesture, but as a desire. It is a powerful force that accompanies the life force and is capable of diverting the destructive judgment that is described as emanating from the fire of the Altar in the Holy Temple.

Ramak brings together our innate tendency to judge with our innate desire for kindness. At the moment of righteous judgment, we remind ourselves of our innate kindness. Ramak asserts that while judgment is an essential component of social order and thus our physicality, the desire to be kind to others is innate. Judgment is a reality of our Nefashot, while kindness extends from and imbues our Neshamot.

Instinctively, we know the value and truth of the power of this combination. Anger and judgment are immediately diverted when we access our kindness. The resulting action, even if it is powered by our judgment, is much more likely to be tempered by consideration of the Other.

Therefore, this middah is a fitting one for human behavior. Even if one is aware that another person has done something bad and is angry; if the person has some good redeeming quality, e.g. she is benevolent to others, or she possesses some other good trait with which she conducts herself righteously – this good side of her should be sufficient for one to nullify one's anger against her and to have a positive feeling towards her and to desire her kindness and say, "It is enough for me that she has this good quality." How much more so does all this apply to one's spouse; as our Sages explained: "It is enough that they raise our children and save us from sin." So, too, one should say with regard to every person, "It is enough that he has done for me or someone else such-and-such a favor, or that he has a such-and-such positive quality," and he should always be "desirous of kindness."

Practicing the middah of "cultivating kindness" means allowing Ruach's compulsion to kindness to be manifested as our own and transferred to the Others in our lives, especially our closest Others. We need this middah when we are angry, having been wronged by another. We remind ourselves of our obligation to see just *one* good quality in the Other – and this observation has the power to return us to our desire to be kind. Once we have practiced with those we know, we move to embodying this middah to the whole world. Ramak intimates that our judgmental feelings are wakeup calls, reminding us of our obligation to recognize and emulate the kindness that courses through this Other as it courses through all the world.

Holiness and Ra are not opposites, but interrelated. For our Tikkun work, Ra is a gateway to *Tov*. Our Nefesh is alive, constantly responding to and interpreting our environment. Being alive means being in relationship with Ra. As long as we live, we will know Ra. We embody holiness as we recognize the Ra inside of us as a wakeup call to soften our rigid Nefesh and/or firm up our overly porous Nefesh and transform the Yetzer from Ra to Tov.

This middah is a guide to moving away from Ra by connecting with kindness, which is a specific aspect of Tov. The middah focuses on the aspects of Ra that manifest when we feel wronged, angry and/or rightly judgmental towards an "evildoer." Like the previous middah, this one guides us to use this experience of Ra as a reminder of our desire for kindness, and then focus on one good deed of the "evildoer."

Practicing this middah can be a challenge. No matter how much we know about the goodness of the Ruach, the flow of the Neshamah and the semi-permeability of the Nefesh, we will inevitably find ourselves in situations where others wrong us. We are likely to plunge into a state of righteous indignation, feeling ourselves sparked to legitimate anger, our brains whirling as we judge the Other. Working this middah means using those judgmental patterns of thought as a signal to check the state of our Nefesh. Let's take it step by step.

When you are wronged and legitimately angry

To practice this middah, we must familiarize ourselves with our own particular brand of thoughts and body sensations when we are judging others and/or ourselves. For some, it begins with a subtle tightening of the jaw, or perhaps a thought like, "What? *What?*" that builds upon itself and, if left alone, will build into a rampage of righteously indignant thoughts. Our thoughts are judge and jury; the defendant is clearly guilty. For others, the judgment is levied against ourselves. This describes those whose

Nefesh is overly porous. Wherever your judgment falls on the spectrum, use this experience to wake up.

Remember your innate desire for kindness

When we work this *middah*, simply waking up will not be enough. We must then take the step of reminding ourselves that we desire kindness. Often this will be a small voice, dwarfed by the judgmental diatribe. Simply remember your desire for kindness and allow yourself to ponder whether you believe kindness is innate. This should interrupt the avalanche of negative thoughts. Do not expect that you can actually embody kindness. The important work is knowing it is possible. The final step in the practice takes us to embodiment.

Allow one good quality of the Other to penetrate you

Acknowledging one good deed has the power to change everything. The dynamic verbs used here – "allow" and "penetrate" — are key. This is no passive exercise, but one which requires active thought. Judgment and anger are only possible with either a rigid or porous Nefesh. "Allowing" means gently letting go of the anger and judgment against the Other or yourself.

MIDDAH SEVEN: COMPASSION

Yeshuv Yirachamenu (God Will Again
Have Compassion Upon Us)

*Allow for a deeper appreciation and closeness with those you
have forgiven than those who have never wronged you.*

The Holy Blessed One does not behave the
way flesh and blood does. When one has been
angered by his friend, when they reconcile,
the reconciliation is minimal and does not
fully restore the love between them to what
it was before. Yet if a person transgresses and
then does teshuvah, the person gains a higher
standing in the eyes of the Holy Blessed One.

In other words, "In the place where a
person who did teshuvah stands, even

complete tzaddikim cannot stand." The sages
explain the reason for this in the "building"
section of tractate "Shabbath": concerning the
letter ה ('hey'), "why is it shaped like a porch?
So that anyone who wants to go astray from the
world may leave." Meaning that the world was
created by means of the letter ה and the Holy
Blessed One created it with a gaping opening
to the side of evil and sin so that nowhere is one
safe from self-absorption, the Yetzer HaRa and
other flaws. Just like a porch, it does not have
an enclosing fence but is breached open in the
lower part, the side of evil. Thus, anyone who
wants to leave from God's world has several
openings available — whichever way the person
turns there is an opening toward the side of
trespass and transgression through which s/he
can enter the realm of Outside God's desired
world.

Yet there is also an upper opening, through
which one may return and be received. Yet the
sages still asked: "And why should the person
not return by the same way s/he went out?" and
answered: "Because this will be of no help." By
this they meant that for the person engaged
in teshuvah, the fences that would protect
a tzaddik from transgression are not enough,
since for a tzaddik, who did not transgress,
smaller fences would suffice. However, for
the person who transgressed and then engages
in teshuvah, such a small fence is not enough,
sturdier fences are needed. This is because for
such a person the smaller fences have already

been breached once and if they are approached again, the Yetzer HaRa will easily tempt the person. The person therefore has to keep far away from that place and not try to re-enter through the same opening that was already breached, but rather climb up and enter through the narrow opening above and thus mend the breaches.

The discussion of the *middah* begins by relating compassion to forgiveness. For us as human beings, forgiving does not automatically mean forgetting. Even when we totally forgive someone, the quality of our relationship is often tinged by the infraction. The quality that bridges between the Infinite Goodness of the universe and the human expression of forgiveness is what Ramak refers to as compassion. For Ramak, the metaphor of the Holy One stands in for Infinite Goodness. According to the Rabbis, the relationship between Infinite Goodness with one who repents (the ba'al teshuvah) is even dearer than the relationship with one who never sins (the tzaddik). This is not to discount the role of perfect tzaddikim in the spiritual infrastructure of our world, for it is said that the lamed vav (36) tzaddikim (righteous ones) or the tzaddikim nestarim (secret righteous ones) hold up the world. Rather, it is to honor the paradox of the middah of compassion in identifying sin and repentance as pathways to drawing even closer to the Divine.

Ramak consistently teaches that Yetzer HaRa is an essential part of the "the blueprint" of Being. Still, the Ramak's choice of the Midrash that posits the world was created with the Hebrew letter hei (ה) adds something of great value to our understanding of what it means to be spiritually embodied.

Ramak's interpretation of this midrash expresses how easy it is for a Nefesh to rigidify and how comparatively more difficult it is to soften it. The image of the letter hei, with its wide gap along the bottom open to "escape" and its narrow squeeze of a side opening for "return," can be read as image of the Nefesh's process. The starting point of an embodied life is a point of consciousness or Neshama. The image of the hei represents the Neshama coming into consciousness of being enclosed inside a Nefesh. The escape or fall begins as the Nefesh moves out of semi-permeability in a mistaken attempt to protect the precious Neshamah. As the constrained Yetzer becomes Ra, the open bottom of the hei cannot contain the "weight" of a Yetzer that believes its rigid or overly porous Nefesh boundary is necessary for protection. In Ramak's imagery, the Yetzer HaRa escapes from the gap in the bottom of the hei.

The Nefesh, embodiment itself, requires the wide-open space of self-perceived freedom to fulfill the intention of creation, which is to increase holiness through greater intimacy with the Divine, the promise offered by teshuva (repentance). Our meaning here is that teshuva is the very purpose of creation. The first exercise of this freedom, "escape" from knowledge of Ruach or holiness, helps to establish the potential "return" to Ruach that is penitence. Thus the penitent person is more highly praised than the tzaddik who has never left home.

At the same time, one who "returns" home does not re-enter through the wide open door by which he or she left. The penitent must squeeze through the small opening toward the top of the hei. It was easy to inflate ourselves and fill the wide open space outside the hei, impervious to Infinite Goodness. Therefore the return requires the more difficult work of contracting ourselves to embrace humility and open ourselves to gratitude for our experience of Infinite Goodness.

And it is for this reason that "In the place where a person who did teshuvah stands, even complete tzaddikim cannot stand": Since they did not enter through the same entrance as the tzaddikim,

they cannot stand together with the tzaddikim. They constrained and disciplined themselves to go up and enter through the upper opening and separated themselves from transgression through much greater constraint and self-discipline than the tzaddikim. In doing this, they have ascended to stand at the level of ה, the fifth palace of the Garden of Eden and the roof of the ה, while the tzaddikim stand at the lower opening of the ה at the entrance of the *exedra* (porch).

Therefore, when a person does teshuvah, meaning returning the ה to its rightful place and returns to the Holy Blessed One. The person does not return to the same love as it was at first, but to a constantly expanding love. In other words, "God will again have compassion upon us" meaning that God will increase her compassion, mend and draw Israel even closer.

Complete tzaddikim are those who can maintain the semi-permeability of their Nefashot. On the other hand, the ba'al teshuva has experienced the impact on self and Other of a porous or rigid Nefesh. They must always be aware of the state of their Nefesh, aware of the necessity to wake up, and allow the flow of Neshama. And for this awakening, the ba'al teshuva is blessed with increased intimacy with the Divine and increased joy in being of service to others.

This is how a person should behave with others. A person should not harbor a grudge from former anger. Rather, when a person sees that a fellow asks for love, the person's love and compassion

for this fellow should reach a much higher level than before. The person should say: "To me this fellow is like those who did teshuva: where they stand even complete tzaddikim cannot stand" and then draw close, closer than to those the person considers complete tzaddikim, because they did not transgress against him/her.

We are taught to recognize when another is sincerely trying to do teshuva, and we emulate the Divine by reaching out to assist that person in his or her efforts. One way to do this is to not dwell on the acts of that person's Yetzer HaRa, but rather celebrate every instance of his or her Yetzer HaTov in action.

In our journey to holiness, the link between forgiveness and compassion is not always a given. We have all experienced a moment when we see someone we've forgiven. Just labeling this person as "forgiven" carries with it the memory of the wrong and the anger that precipitated the forgiveness. This increases the potential for our Nefesh membrane to rigidify or become porous.

The middah guides us to use moments when we view this Other as someone we have forgiven as a wakeup call, a reminder of our commitment to embody holiness. The wakeup call is noticing our inclination to still see this Other as someone who has been forgiven for wronging us. Ramak's conception of the middah of compassion asks us to open our hearts even further to this person. How? By acknowledging the intimate relationship between ourselves and this person whose Yetzer HaRa has impacted us.

This connection between people who affect each others' Yetzrot goes even deeper. When someone else's changing Nefesh triggers ours, it is no accident. We are like two pieces of a jigsaw puzzle finding each other. The Ra created by this person's rigid or semi porous Nefesh fits perfectly with the Ra created by our responding Nefesh. Consequently we are both perfectly trapped in our steadily rigidifying (or porous) Nefeshot. Every action of our friend perfectly solidifies our feelings of separation and vice versa.

The work of this middah is recognizing the familiar wakeup call of the Yetzer HaRa. We know the call is specific to us: We are "chosen" to be the ones who will break the cycle, even if we've already forgiven. Practicing this middah means when we see this other, we wake up to our shared intimacy. We two are perfectly formed so our Yetzer HaRa can accomplish the miraculous. Theirs wakes us to the Divine, and we then encircle theirs with Yetzer HaTov.

Seen through this lens, it is easy to feel gratitude for the expansion that their Yetzer HaRa's expression has offered to us. After all, their Yetzer HaRa woke us to a new and, until then, unknown path to holiness. We greet this Other with deep acknowledgement for the "miracle" of our aligned Yetzerot. We know that this is the Divine design for our embodied spirits: to wake each other up to holiness. And in that we two are closer because it is only together that we can journey through this merciful life.

MIDDAH EIGHT: TRANSFORMATION

Yichbosh avonoteinu (He will suppress our iniquities)

Look only for the Good

The Holy Blessed One behaves toward Israel according to this middah, which is the secret of suppressing iniquity. For a mitzvah is like a bud when it bursts into bloom, shooting up and rising beyond all bounds to enter before the Blessed One. Iniquities, however, do not gain entry there, God forbid. God suppresses them so they will not be able to enter, as is written, "Evil will not dwell with you," (Psalms 5:5) which is to say "evil shall not dwell with You in Your place of dwelling." Thus iniquities do not permeate the Divine. This is the reason why

"the reward of a mitzvah is not in this world,"
(Kiddushin 39b) because they do permeate
the Blessed One. Then how is it possible for
these spiritual rewards to be translated into the
material world, when this world is not the place
for spiritual rewards to be granted?

The dimension of existence that our tradition names "Olam Hazeh," this world, we take to be a metaphor for the experience of self-absorption. In our approach, Olam Hazeh and Olam Haba, the world to come, are dimensions of experience that are available to us at every moment. We are in Olam Hazeh when our Nefeshot are porous or rigid, and we approach Olam Haba as we use mitzvot as vehicles to semi-permeability and experience the joy of Neshamot connecting with each other. Ramak clarifies for us in this section that "mitzvot," deeds that either interrupt our self-absorption or make real our impulse to serve another, cannot, by definition, "exist" in "Olam Hazeh." On the contrary, they are precisely the conditions that bring us to an experience of "Olam Haba." Similarly, self-absorption and its consequences (iniquities) do not exist in Olam Haba.

This is the reason why God will not take
mitzvot for bribes. For instance, the Holy
Blessed One does not say, God forbid: "She
did forty mitzvot and ten transgressions: there
are still thirty mitzvot left after we deduct
ten transgressions for ten mitzvot." For even
a complete tzaddik who commits a single
transgression is considered as if he had burnt
the Torah until he has reconciled his debt, after
which he receives the reward for all his mitzvot.
This is the great kindness that the Holy Blessed
One does for the tzaddikim: God does not

subtract from the mitzvot, since they have great importance and they ascend until they come into the Blessed Presence. Indeed, how could God subtract mitzvot to match transgressions, since the compensation for transgression partakes of Gehinom (*commonly translated as purgatory*), of what is most despicable, while the compensation for mitzvot partakes of the radiance of God's Presence, of what is most honorable. Then how could God subtract these to match those? Rather, God collects the debt owed for transgressions and repays the reward accrued for all the mitzvot.

It is for this reason we cannot compare mitzvot with averot (transgressions), nor calculate a relationship between the two: They exist in two separate dimensions. Averot have consequences independent of how many mitzvot we perform and the rewards of mitzvot are not tainted by the averot we commit. We understand the use of the word Gehinom to metaphorically describe the internal suffering experienced by one who is self-absorbed.

This is the meaning of "God will repress our iniquities:" that the iniquities do not increase in strength before God like mitzvot. Rather, God represses them so they will not rise and gain entry. Even though God supervises all the ways of people, good and bad, nevertheless the good is never repressed, but rather blossoms and rises up high, mitzvah upon mitzvah weaving together like the threads of a precious garment. Yet transgressions do not have this capability: Rather, God represses them so they

will not succeed in entering the inner precincts of the Divine.

The difference between the rewards of mitzvot and the consequences of averot is that the mitzvot are endowed with the power of expansiveness. That is, the Neshama, the source of mitzvot, expands, permeating through the enclosure of the Nefesh to fill the space between one person and the other. Averot, on the other hand, remain attached only to the deeds that created them, the particular element of Nefesh-defensiveness that engendered them.

A person has to behave according to this middah as well, by not suppressing another's good deeds while recalling the evil the person has committed. Rather, on the contrary, the evil should be suppressed, forgotten and relinquished, so that "evil shall not dwell" within; and the good should be kept in mind and be constantly remembered so the good prevails over all the deeds that this other person does. One should not subtract from them by saying: "Although this other did me good, and also did me wrong" and thus forget about the good. One should not do this, but rather use every available way to reconcile with the evil done by another while never losing sight of the good. One should overlook the evil as much as one can, just the way the Holy Blessed One represses iniquities, as we have explained.

Since the dimension of holiness is expanded by mitzvot and not contracted by averot, so too we emulate the Holy One as we allow our fellow's mitzvot, their Yetzer HaTov actions, to grow. We recognize their Neshama as it expands through their Nefesh and see it filling the space and intermingling with our own Neshamah. We are one. At the same time, we do not allow their averot, their Yetzer HaRa deeds, to penetrate into our Nefesh or excite our Yetzer HaRa. Our tradition defines this dynamic as imitating the Divine.

With this the eighth attribute, Ramak finally clarifies what we have suspected all along: that the choice given to us by Moses in Deuteronomy chapter 19 — *I put before you life and death, blessing and curse, choose life* — is not only a true choice, it is truly our purpose, our duty, our ultimate form of *imatatio Dei*.

Evil, or the Yetzer HaRa, is a necessary part of our embodied sojourn. But once we know evil for what it is — a wake up call to our Neshama — then it is our obligation to do all we can to not increase that energy in any way, shape or form. That means doing everything in our power to not join with anything that carries with it any seed of Yetzer HaRa. Our moral imperative is: Look only for the good. Seeing only the good is a form of *imatatio Dei*. In this middah, the Ramak goes so far as to suggest that we train ourselves to repress Yetzer HaRa by starving it of our energy and attention. It is this simple. If we notice Yetzer HaRa, and spend even an iota of our precious attention on it, its energy grows. But if we experience Yetzer HaRa from a neutral distance, simply noting that there is Yetzer HaRa in our field, we can then move our attention kindly, easily to something else — to noticing and then expanding the good.

As we do this, we (and our Others) expand our ability to notice Yetzer HaTov, and grow our ability to remember

MIDDAH NINE: RADICAL LOVING EQUANIMITY

V'Tashlich B'Mtzolot yam kol Chatotam (And you will cast all their iniquities into the depths of the sea)

Maintain loving equanimity to the mystery of a world with sin, and bring close those who suffer for their sins

Because of the flow of Ramak's commentary on this middah, we present his words in full and will comment in full below.

This is a good middah of the Holy Blessed One. Since Israel sinned, God delivered them into the hands of Pharaoh; yet when Israel repented, why does God punish Pharaoh, or for that matter, Sanheriv, Haman and their like? The Holy Blessed One is not content just to say: "They did repent, so no evil will befall them

anymore and Haman, Pharaoh or Sanheriv will be removed from them. It does not end there, rather the labor of Haman will revert upon his own head, and so too with Pharaoh and Sanheriv.

The reason for this conduct is in the mystery of "and the goat shall bear upon him all their iniquities unto a land which is cut off" (VaYikra 16:22). The meaning is that the goat actually bears their iniquities, but this raises a difficulty: If Israel committed the iniquities, how come it is the goat that has to bear them? Now here is how to understand this middah: When a person confesses, her intention in doing so is to be cleansed, as David said: "Cleanse me thoroughly of my iniquity" (Psalms 51:4). And we say in our prayers: "Erase with your great compassion." All the person prays for is that the afflictions be light, by saying: "And not by means of harsh afflictions," so they won't lead to abandoning Torah study. As the prayer continues, this is also the intention behind the words: "You are righteous concerning anything that befalls me." The person genuinely welcomes the afflictions in order to atone, because there are iniquities that only afflictions or death can cleanse. This is how the middah manifests itself: right after one has confessed, as the Zohar on parashat Pekudei explains, the sin becomes the portion of Samael (the angel of evil), who is represented by the goat. What exactly is Samael's portion? That when the Holy Blessed One decrees suffering upon a person, Samael shows up there immediately to collect his due. By doing so, with the permission of the Holy Blessed One, Samael takes on the iniquities and Israel is cleansed of them. Thus everything migrates upon Samael. The reason is that the Holy Blessed One decreed upon the world that whoever acts like this will be annihilated. This is why it is written: "The animal shall be killed [referring to the goat]" (Vayikra 20:15). Similarly, the stone used to fulfill the commandment of execution by stoning and the sword used to fulfill the commandment of execution by beheading, are supposed to be buried in order to annihilate their existence and power after they have carried out the sentence.

This is the mystery of Nebuchadnessar's statue: Israel was delivered into the hands of the king of Babylon, the "head of gold." That head was defeated and they were delivered into the hands of Persia, who are the "breasts and arms of silver." Thus, one kept getting overthrown by the other until Israel found themselves down by the "feet, part iron, part clay." Now what would be a good ending to this? In the end, they will stand trial before the Holy Blessed One, as is written, "I spent my arrows on them" or "my arrows will be spent, yet Israel will not be spent."

"Then the iron, the clay, the bronze, the silver and the gold were all broken to pieces" (Daniel 2:35). First it is written, "It struck the statue on its feet": nothing was left of the statue but its feet. All the rest, head, arms, breast had been eliminated and their power nullified. Yet still, in the end we are told that they "were all broken to pieces." For the Holy Blessed One will have Samael and the wicked who carry out Samael's actions and works stand trial.

This is the meaning of "You will cast all their iniquities into the depths of the sea," in other words, You will cast the power of judgment to work against those who in Isaiah are called "the depths of the sea." "And the wicked are like the troubled sea, for it cannot rest and its waters cast up mire and dirt" (Isaiah 57:20). This refers to those who carry out judgment against Israel and whose actions will fall back upon their heads. This is because after Israel has received that sanction, the Holy Blessed One regrets what has happened and demands reparation for the insult they suffered. And moreover, "I was angered a little, and they helped make it worse" (Zechariah 1:15).

A person should behave toward her fellow according to this middah too: even if the fellow is wicked and weighed down by suffering, she should not hate the person because "after being demeaned, he is like your brother." She should bring close those who have been brought low by punishment and have mercy on them. She should go even further and rescue them from the hand of their enemy and not say: "It is because of their sins," but rather show the person mercy according to this middah, as I have explained.

In this middah, Ramak relates one of the most consistent metaphors in biblical and later Jewish tradition. It is the story of Israel sinning, God punishing Israel through the actions of an evil empire, God hearing Israel's cries, God defeating the enemy and causing that enemy to suffer. Here, Ramak is concerned with why these evil enemies are punished after they have done what is essentially God's will. In order to understand the metaphor in a contemporary context, we must translate it into the language we are developing. We understand 'God' to stand for a system that has the potential for holiness. The system contains within it a set of dynamics that provides choice points for people who have free will and can choose sin or holiness. The choice made by the so-called evil nations in the story is their choice, triggered by Israel's sin, but independent of it. When Israel repents the evil nations still must make their own choice to repent. When they don't, we call the results "their punishment." In this system dynamic we understand sin to be self-absorption and the resulting Nefesh that is either overly porous or rigid. 'Punishment' is the pain inflicted upon us by the others with whom we engage, who by our actions are triggered into this state.

If we could cull all the Tikkun middot practices into one, it would be: Imitate God by continuing to "sustain and nourish in Divine Goodness" (see middah 1 and 2). From the first middah to this one, the middot are so counterintuitive that they might cause us to abandon this stance. Whenever we perceive evil in the world, whether we find ourselves judging a perpetrator or mourning for an innocent victim; whether the evil is writ large (murder or genocide) or writ small (arriving late to an appointment), we are urged to maintain this stance.

Our mission when we perceive evil or the impact of evil is to connect with the potential for choosing yetzer hatov and abandon any attachment to the yetzer hara. This is how we influence God, or the system. We put our energy into yetzer hatov and no energy into yetzer hara and in this way we are "God's agents."

In addition we read this particular biblical metaphor as suggesting an idea we have not encountered previously, the idea of mass yetzer hara. Haman, Sanheriv and Pharoah had a propensity towards self-absorption, and chose to act on that propensity which gave license for the yetzer hara behavior of their populations. This directs our attention to the reality that yetzer hara energy can infect whole groups and the contagion can exist at the societal level. We take Ramak's choice of talking about nations as opposed to the single human beings he has referenced in previous middot, to signify Ramak's desire to bring to our awareness that these 'rules' of how yetzer works are universal and happen at the individual, group and national level. Thus Ramak uses the biblical story to reinforce the idea of God as a system within which yetzer hara--holiness is always a potential choice point for individuals and nations.

We believe, as Ramak does, that these stories teach us about how Yetzer works in this world. When in the story Israel repents, or returns to a state of flowing Neshama, that return didn't diminish their oppressors' self-absorption. We understand this to mean that even when a person turns from self-absorption, the impact of their having been self-absorbed does not disappear from the world. Thus Ramak learns from this that "cleansing" is not the total erasure of the consequences of our actions that stem from self-absorption. Regardless of the process of atonement, the consequences of our actions remain and their impact endures. This is represented by the fact that Israel's repentance did not cause her enemies to repent.

Whereas the first midrashim dealt with the predicament of the oppressor, the second series of midrashim deal with the predicament of the oppressed. Since Israel was the catalyst triggering the self-absorptive tendencies of their oppressors, Ramak asks the question: Despite Israel's repentance, does Israel have a responsibility toward her enemies? The always present imperative to serve the other is no less present in these seemingly extreme scenarios. Israel's responsibility is to stay in her yetzer hatov. The choice for her enemies is whether they stay in their yetzer hara or move back toward their own yetzer hatov. To reiterate, this system dynamic is part of what we understand as 'God,' the ever-expanding journey and the potential for holiness.

In the metaphor of the text, this is exemplified by God's assignment of their sinfulness to Samael. Samael is often called the 'evil angel,' but is actually the agent God (or the system) whose task is to collect, in this case Israel's sin, after she has repented, in order to limit its effects, by placing it on the Yom Kippur goat and leading the goat into the wilderness. In this way the system processes sins and returns to a state of atonement. While the destruction of the goat may not appear to us initially as an act of compassion, Ramak equates it with the stone or sword used to kill the guilty. Like these tools, this sin must also be hidden from the world. Thus he is suggesting that "God" or the system, cannot erase evil, but God can banish its effects. Ramak uses these particular metaphors — Samael, the evil creature created by our deeds (see middah 2); and the goats used in the Yom Kippur ritual for atonement — to understand why those who awaken us and allow us to return to semi-permeability may themselves continue to suffer until they too can be awakened.

Through this middah, Ramak confirms the reality that when we awaken and reestablish our semi-permeable Nefesh, others around us may still be trapped in their self-absorption. It then becomes our responsibility to bear them with a semi-permeable Nefesh. If we don't, we are likely to be triggered and fall back into self-absorption.

Second, the middah provides us with a lens from which to observe the suffering of others. Witnessing suffering requires an even stronger effort to maintain the permeability of our Nefesh. We must strive to be available to the one who suffers without inflicting pain or experiencing pain. Finally, as Ramak emphasizes, we should encounter the seemingly wicked individual as well as those who suffer innocently with the utmost mercy and love.

We become aware that the increase of yetzer hatov in the world is not always visible. Working this middah, we maintain the semi-permeability of our Nefesh regardless. We cultivate the awareness that nothing is truly broken because the world is set up so that there is always the potential to choose holiness. We work this middah by reminding ourselves that whenever we hear anything that we might judge as Ra, as 'evil,' we know that holiness is a an available choice, that Ra is the wakeup call. We do this until it becomes automatic. When we hear about something negative, we are vigilant in noticing whether our immediate reaction includes a change in our Nefesh boundary. If we feel a change, we invoke this middah as a reminder of the mystery of holiness that cannot be seen.

In relation to our others, we practice moving from judgment to seeing the possibilities of holiness. It is a choice. We could hear about the perpetrators of genocide. We could hear about the innocent victims. We could hear about the misdeeds of our neighbors. None of it is cause to move out of semi-permeability. Of course, that does not mean we cannot take action against the wrongs of the world — in fact we *must* precisely because we must choose tov over ra. And action from love is required. This middah confirms what we know, that there is never a reason to abandon our commitment to maintaining a semi-permeable *Nefesh*. Period.

MIDDAH TEN: TRUTH

Titain Emet L'Ya'akov (Grant truth to Ya'akov)

Be guided by truth, differences exist, it is not ours to judge

This middah teaches that there is a dimension within the nation Israel that applies to average people who do not know how to behave beyond the requirements of the law. They are called Ya'akov because they only behave according to the literal truth. The Holy One also has this dimension of truth. Those who conduct themselves according to the law and uprightness, the Holy Blessed One behaves towards them with truth, has mercy on them in a way that is upright and just.

Also, a person should behave towards his/her fellow from the perspective of uprightness and truth, without tipping the scales. Just as the Holy Blessed One has compassion on those of God's creatures who are average and rectifies them in order to perfect them, so should a person be compassionate towards his/her fellows in truth.

With this middah, Ramak teaches that if we've practiced the previous middot, we've learned enough about how to position ourselves in relation to the reality that evil exists in the world. We are now ready to learn how to position ourselves in relation to the good in the world.

In this and the next middah, Ramak uses the rubrics of Ya'akov and Avraham to talk about the reality that there are different levels of spiritual attainment. The meaning of the term Ya'akov describes those who act according to the letter of the law and conventional morality. They are not swayed unduly by emotion, nor prejudiced by their own interests. They hold themselves and others accountable for their actions. Many good people are satisfied to live at the level of Ya'akov, following the rules and laws, going about their business and striving to act correctly.

We've come far in our pursuit of holiness. By now we are committed to this path and aware of its vitality and its importance. This middah reminds us that not everyone's soul path takes them beyond the level of Ya'akov. As we continue on our journey we recognize that we must maintain our anavah, humility, continuing to see everyone, as our teacher.

This middah brings out our responsibility to remain in a state of semi-permeability without expecting the Other to also actively cultivate holiness. Ramak combines the two middot of Emet (truth) and Rachamim (compassion) to guide us in accepting the truth of how this world is created: that there are differences in each person's soul path, and spiritual attainment is but one way. The middah warns against self-righteousness and holding ourselves and our holy curriculum as morally superior to Others. Rather we are to be guided by the qualities of truth and compassion, and to always remember that while differences exist, it is not for us judge.

MIDDAH ELEVEN:
KINDHEARTEDNESS

Chesed L'Avraham (Kindness to Avraham)

*Surround yourself with people and experiences
that align with your quest for holiness.*

These are the ones whose behavior goes
beyond the letter of the law, like Avraham our
patriarch. With them The Holy Blessed One
also acts beyond the letter of the law. God does
not summon against them the strictness or even
uprightness of judgment, but rather goes with
them beyond uprightness, just as they do with
others. This is the meaning of "kindness to
Avraham": that the Holy Blessed One behaves
with the middah of kindness (chesed) towards
those who behave like Avraham.

> This applies to people too: Even if a person
> acts within the confines of what is just, upright
> and lawful in general, toward those who are
> particularly good and kind, the person's conduct
> should go beyond the letter of the law. As she
> displays patience when dealing with people in
> general, she should have even more patience and
> compassion towards the good and the kind and
> go beyond the letter of the law with them. These
> people should be very precious and beloved to
> her and be part of her close companions.

Ramak describes the Divine as acting with kindheartedness towards those who exhibit kindness in their dealings with others. Just as they go beyond the letter of the law, beyond what is required by justice, so too are they treated by the Holy One beyond the measure of strict justice.

Ramak's interpretation is striking in that it distinguishes between Jewish identity and something greater. In the previous middah, Ramak identifies Ya'akov with the Jewish people presumably because Ya'akov is the only patriarch whose children constitute the totality of the Israelite nation. People who are identfied as Ya'akov are those who are ruled by law (halacha)those who use the rules about how we treat each other as the route to "good enough" behavior. According to the rabbis, following these rules for the sake of being a good person is not only enough, it is a noble end in itself. It prevents those who seek holiness from forsaking attending to the good of others while pursuing that holiness. Implicit in Ramak's concept of Yaakov is that the pursuit of holiness does not free one from the obligations of law.

Holiness always exists through our relationships with others. Rules become the structure within which we cultivate that holiness. A truth about the Jewish path to holiness is that it is predicated on a person continuing to "follow the rules." There is not a time where the rules become inconsequential. Rather, the rules become the anchor that prevents us from seeking God at the expense of people. Grounded in these rules, some will be inspired to pursue a holiness that transcends "good enough," a level of holiness where kindheartedness is cultivated. This is the level of Avraham.

This level of holiness is not restricted to just the Jewish people. Remember, Avraham's two sons, encompass Israel, *and* the descendents of Yishmael, that is, the Israelite *and* non Israelite world. This is a clear indication that holiness transcends and should not be conflated with national or ethnic identities.

The Avrahamic spiritual path to holiness invites us to go beyond the letter of the law. For Ramak, Avraham — who discerned monotheism for all the nations of the world — signifies a higher moral status than Ya'akov. Avraham, who first charted a path to holiness through the One God, is presented as having an unremitting focus on kindness in his relationships with others. This is the Avraham's manifestation of his spiritual vision and his understanding of the Divine: Kindness to others is holiness. From this we learn that holiness and love of others are synonymous.

This culminates a series of three middot that gives us a new lens through which to view our relationships with different kinds of people, and asks us to explore our own behavior. Middah Nine prompts us to believe in the healing rather than the brokenness of those in their Ra. Middah ten guides our behavior to people, here designated as Ya'akov, who do not search for holiness; we are not meant to judge them, but rather to relate to them through humility. Middah 11 is a guide to how we encounter the people who prioritize their spiritual quest. We recognize them as part of our spiritual community and hold them close.

This middah focuses our attention on the people we surround ourselves with. Who do we consider our close companions? While we are asked to think well of all people, our close companions should be those who, like Avraham, extend themselves to bring kindness and generosity to the world. "Close companions" does not imply people who we *happen* to spend our time with. "Close companions" refer to those who, like us, are on a quest to expand holiness. Whether we come into contact with them for a minute, an hour, or a lifetime, we are meant to cherish and be nourished by their companionship, regardless of their ethnic, national or religious orientation. Ramak asks us to notice what lifts us up as we seek to embody holiness. Certainly this includes people, but we are also guided to cherish other kinds of companions; those we make of the books we read, the music we listen to, the nature we revel in or the art we admire.

The middah suggests that we surround ourselves with people and experiences that support our quest for holiness. It is a reflective middah. It gives us the opportunity to take stock of how we spend our time, and to ask ourselves: Who and what am I choosing to influence me? Who around me has consciously committed themselves to holiness? How do I hold them close? And how do those relationships sustain and nourish my spiritual journey?

MIDDAH TWELVE: LEGACY

Asher Nishbatah L'Avotenu (As You Promised to our Ancestors)

*Trust in the legacy of our ancestors, and
treat the wicked with kindness*

There are people who are unworthy and yet the
Holy Blessed One has mercy upon them. The
Gemara explains the verse: "I will be gracious
to whom I will be gracious" as that the Holy
One says: "This storehouse is for those who
are unworthy." There is a storehouse of grace
from which the Holy Blessed One gives them an
unearned gift. For the Holy One says: "Behold
they possess the merit of the ancestors. I have
made an oath to the Patriarchs, therefore
even if they are not worthy they shall receive
their reward because they are the seed of the

Patriarchs to whom I have sworn. I will lead them, therefore, and direct them until they improve."

So, too, should a person behave. Even when she meets with the wicked she should not behave cruelly towards them nor insult them but have mercy upon them saying: "Even so, they are the children of Avraham, Yitzchak and Yaakov [Sarah, Rivkah, Rachel and Leah]. If they are not worthy their ancestors were worthy and upright and he who brings disgrace upon the children brings disgrace upon the ancestors and I have no wish that the ancestors be despised through me." And she should conceal their shame and improve them as much as is in her power.

How are we to act when confronted with people who appear truly undeserving of our kindness and compassion? This is the final class of people with whom we will inevitably have contact: those who are, or appear to be, irremediably evil. Their Neshamot are truly hidden — that is, their Nefesh boundaries seem to be permanently rigid or porous.

When we practice this middah we are practicing faith and transcendence. Only when we reach near the end of the 13 middot are we finally prepared for the obligation this middah brings. We are required to treat even the truly wicked with kindness because all of humanity has accumulated a treasury of kindness based on the relationship between the Divine and the founding ancestors of human ethical insight. That is, Avraham and Sarah's initial insight that the obligation to serve the Other is infinitely extended; Yitzchak and Rivka's imperative to keep closest those who are with us on the spiritual path; Ya'akov, Rachel and Leah's insight that people who are not on a search for greater spiritual understanding still merit being treated with truth and compassion. As a result of these insights, a fountain of open-heartedness came into being in the world that is available even to the most wicked. Due to this fountain, we can act toward those whom, without this "Divine intercession," our response would be judgmental, resulting in acts of vengeance and cruelty. Our response to pure irredeemable evil has been the proverbial "elephant in the room" throughout our encounter with the radical theology of Ramak. Here he at last invites us to grapple with it and be transformed.

The middah, called Asher Nishbatah L'Avotenu, "As promised to our ancestors" and the treasury that Ramak derives from it, is a metaphor signaling that each one of us is connected to those who came before us — that what we do relates to them and what they did relates to us. That what seems like many neshamot is really one neshamah only experienced individually. How our Neshamot and our Nefashot are related to each other and to those who lived before and after is part of the mystery we cannot know. It is with this mystery as a backdrop that we are guided to respond to the "wicked" with the unearned gift of kindness.

We are guided to see wicked people as distressed, and as related to others who have a close relationship to the Divine. These wicked ones are the distressed children of holy people. Thus we do what we can to actively ease their distress, and make sure not to further contribute to it.

We practice this middah every time we hear of wickedness in the world, and use the middah as a guide to our behavior in response to evil. We do not condone the wicked behavior. Our choice is about how we react to it. We need to choose a reaction that in no way mimics or amplifies the wicked behavior. Therefore, when we can offer rebuke to the evil behavior of others, we do so from our wellspring of kindness, rather than from anger. This is the stance from which rebuke and resistance comes. Our Tradition's standard is that a rebuke of someone's actions can only be effective when offered with love and received by the Other as a gift.

MIDDAH THIRTEEN: HOLINESS

Mimei Kedem (From Days of Old)

As I behave, so will that quality shine upon earth

This is a quality that the Holy One, Blessed Be, possesses with regard to Israel. When, for instance, the merit of their ancestors has come to an end and they are unworthy in themselves, what does God do? It is written (Yirmiyahu 2: 1) "I remember for you the affection of your youth, the love of your espousals." The Holy One, Blessed Be, actually remembers the old times, the former love that existed and has mercy on Israel. In this fashion, God recalls all the Mitzvot Israel has done from the day of their birth and all the good qualities with which the Holy One, Blessed Be, conducts the world.

From all these, God creates a special treasure with which to show mercy to them. This quality embraces all others as the Idra (Zohar ha Kaddosh, Nasso 134b) explains.

So, too, should a person behave. Even when he cannot discover any plea such as those mentioned he should still say: "Behold there was a time when they had not sinned. And in that time or in former days they were worthy." And a person should recall the good they have done in their youth and remember the love of "them that are weaned from the milk, them that are drawn from the breasts." In this way no person will be found an unworthy recipient of goodness nor unworthy to be prayed for and to have mercy shown to him.

This completes our explanation of the thirteen qualities by which a person should emulate the Creator. These are the qualities of higher mercy and their special property is that just as an individual behaves here so will the person be worthy of opening that higher quality from above. As he behaves, so will be the affluence from above and he will cause that quality to shine upon earth. Therefore, let not these thirteen qualities depart from the eyes of the mind and let not the verse depart from the mouth, so that it is a permanent reminder. And whenever there is the opportunity of exercising one of these qualities one will remember, saying to oneself: "Behold, this depends on this particular quality. I shall not depart from it, so

that the quality may not be hidden and depart from the world."

This final middah functions as the crowning middah of the set, and the culmination of the entire chapter. In *Tomer Devorah* Ramak emphasizes the fact that evil is an inevitable product of this world and does not exist in what we call the Divine. The chapter is an exposition of how those who aspire to holiness can respond to this human-made evil. In this final middah, Ramak brings his message home: We are to recognize that the existence of evil, regardless of how rampant, does not diminish the treasury of goodness in the world, which we recognize as the Divine. The implication here is that there is not a link between goodness/evil in the world and the existence of goodness. Goodness *is*.

In our terminology this Divine Goodness is called Ruach which sustains us and our ability to maintain a semi-permiable Nefesh, no matter what we face. This middah demonstrates the infinite nature of Divine goodness as exemplified by the initial act of creation.

Ramak's definition of attaining the highest spiritual level is the capacity to recognize that there exists a quality in every other that solicits a wellspring of kindness from us, simply by their being human. Access to this state is the goal of the entire process described by these middot.

Ramak ends the chapter with the reminder that our purpose is to keep these thirteen middot in our minds and hearts. The people and situations in our lives are opportunities or wake up calls to bring one or more of these Divine qualities into the world. It is the ultimate challenge that Ramak places before us. The Divine depends on us to be made known and thus the purpose of human beings is to channel the Divine into this earthly plane.

Throughout the thirteen middot we learn how to align with the Divine. With this middah, we are reminded that it is our behavior, the quality of our forgiveness and kindness that results in Divine energy shining onto our world. The implication is that the Divine is always Tov. The "cause" of Ra is the closed Nefesh of the human instrument that channels the Divine energy.

Ramak's profound understanding of the relationship between Divine energy and human action is the basis for the development of our contemporary Tikun Mussar practice. Our task is to moment by moment align our actions towards others with these Divine qualities. We practice holding those moments when we do not live up to our aspirations as reminders of what's possible. Ultimately Ramak's work is an incredibly optimistic view of the human experience. It takes the universe of things we deem as evil and non- Godly and makes them a vital component of how we as humans can transform evil into good. It also places increible responsibility on human beings, thus raising up the meaning of being human. We are the vessels for divine energy. And whether the world is good or bad depends on our ability to work with the reality of evil and transform that energy using divinely inspired middot.

ACKNOWLEDGEMENTS

We began this work as a teaching text for the advanced Va'ad that we co-taught as part of the Center for Contemporary Mussar at Temple Beth Zion-Beth Israel in Philadelphia. We are grateful to both institutions for their support. It was our students who led us to look for, to learn and to apply Ramak's work to their longing to be available to the people around them with authenticity, resilience and love. Without their feedback and encouragement there would be no book.

Both of us want to acknowledge our closest "others."

We both learned most of our Mussar from our teachers and partners, Annie Stone and Steve Masters, and are eternally grateful.

To our colleagues on the Mussar journey, we could not have done this without all of you: Mindy Shapiro, Nancy Axelrod, Herb Levine, Rachel Bovitz, Eugene Sotirescu, Sonia Voynow, Carol Daniels, and Linda Kriger, as well as all the Madrichim of the programs of the Center for Contemporary Mussar: Each of you has shared with us how this work has grown your capacity to love -- and that has inspired us in the work of completing this text.

We have been the beneficiaries of the extraordinary editing talents of Sabrina Rubin-Erdely. From her first reading she understood that Ramak's book was not meant to be read, it was meant to inspire each of us to embody the Divine. We thank her for her precision and openness to the real purpose of the work.

No endeavor, even when there are two hands working together, is ever the result of those two people alone. We are deeply grateful to the Divine Spirit, working in the sixteenth century through the words of Rabbi Moshe Cordovero, for giving us the opportunity to bring our twenty first century Mussar rendering to fruition. When we began this journey in the steps of Rabbi Salanter we knew that part of the Mussar ethos is that each generation creates a Mussar practice that meets the needs of their times. The history of holiness in its Jewish garb has always emerged from the conversation across the centuries of those in search of the Source of the Spirit. Ramak's work represents one of the highest expressions of that conversation up to his time. We are humbled and privileged to bring that conversation into our times.

ABOUT THE AUTHORS

Rabbi Ira Stone serves as the Rosh Yeshiva of the Center for Contemporary Mussar. He has served congregations in Seattle, WA, and Philadelphia, PA. He was the spiritual leader at Temple Beth Zion-Beth Israel, Philadelphia, for 27 years and is now Rabbi Emeritus.

Rabbi Stone's first book on mussar is *A Responsible Life: The Spiritual Path to Mussar* (Aviv Press, 2006). His innovative commentary on Rabbi Moshe Hayyim Luzzatto's *Mesillat Yesharim* was published by The Jewish Publication Society in September 2010. With his collaborator, Dr. Beulah Tray, he is currently writing a translation of and commentary on the Mussar classic, Rabbi Moshe Cordovero's *Tomer Devorah*. These commentaries are central to the curriculum of CCM.He is also the author of *Reading Levinas/Reading Talmud* (JPS, 1998), *Seeking the Path to Life* (Jewish Lights, 1993)

Dr. Beulah Trey is a founder of the Center for Contemporary Mussar and Director of Curriculum & Practice, in addition to teaching advanced classes, is responsible for curriculum development and group process training. Born into a South African Jewish family, raised in an orthodox Jewish community, married into a fourth generation reform family, follower of a conservative Rabbi and a member of a Reconstructionist synagogue, finding Mussar has given Beulah a practice that incorporates the diverse paths inside and outside Judaism that have nurtured her soul. Aware of the power of Mussar to transform lives, she pioneers the applications of these practices to leadership, team and organizational transformation.

The Center for Contemporary Mussar was launched in August 2017, as an independent non-profit organization, after more than 15 years as a synagogue-based program (The Mussar Leadership

Program). We offer introductory and continuing classes that focus on Mussar texts, theology and practice. Students commit for a semester at a time; a complete curriculum is offered over a period of four years.

Printed in the United States
By Bookmasters